KIM CAUDLE LEWIS

THE POWER OF *ten* TEN

Terri,
Thank you
for always
supporting
of YA,
Kim

OPPORTUNITIES EVERY LEADER SHOULD LEVERAGE

Limits of Liability and Disclaimer of Warranty

The author and publisher shall not be liable for your misuse of this
material. This book is strictly for informational purposes. The purpose
of this book is to educate and entertain. The author and publisher do
not guarantee anyone following these techniques, suggestions, tips, ideas,
or strategies will become successful. The author and publisher shall
have neither liability nor responsibility to anyone with respect to any loss
or damage caused, or alleged to be caused, directly or indirectly by the
information contained in this book. Views expressed in this publication
do not necessarily reflect the views of the publisher.

Cover: By Triv designsbytriv@gmail.com

Printed in the United States of America
Keen Vision Publishing, LLC
www.publishwithKVP.com
ISBN: 978-1-955316-10-1

For Larry, Flo, Maceo, Charlene, Mary, Maurice, Anthony, Twanda, Sylvia, and Stacy. Thank you for always being supportive, encouraging, and my inspiration.

Charley D. & Lela Mae, thank you for being the best parents.

CONTENTS

INTRODUCTION

As far back as I can remember, my family has always been huge. Yes, people often say that, especially in the African American community, but it is true for me. My immediate family consisted of my parents and nine siblings. NINE! The twelve of us lived on a farm in Triana, Alabama, and while we sometimes had to carve out our own space, the farm was always a place of safety, security, and love.

Growing up in a big family did not necessarily mean we had a tough childhood or an extremely difficult life, but it did mean that things were not often handed to us on a silver platter. There were numerous kids around me, each with various needs that our parents had to tend to, which taught me that I would not always receive things just because I wanted them. My childhood experience played a significant role in preparing me to function in the "real world."

As the youngest of ten children, I was afforded the invaluable opportunity to observe my siblings from a unique vantage point. In a huge family, teasing is inevitable, even if it is mostly good-natured. Siblings tend to pick on each other and sometimes leave each other out. Though it occasionally upset you as a kid, it helped you develop a tough outer layer and taught you how to deal with feelings of discomfort.

We were a close-knit family that took care of each other -- we did not have a choice. Our mom was mentally ill, and no one knew it because, as a family, we decided to deal with it privately. Mental illness was not widely discussed in the African American community in those days. Even now, the topic can be viewed as taboo. Although our mom was mentally ill, she fought to be our mother. She tried her best to do everything mothers should do for their children. We all recognized her fight, so we tried our best to make it as easy for her as possible.

When I say, "We grew up on a farm," I mean a real farm, complete with cows, pigs, and chickens. I even shucked some corn a few times. You are reading a book written by an authentic country girl! In our extended family, we were known as the "country cousins," you know, the ones who didn't have pretty, fancy things. However, we had a lot of love, and for that, I am eternally grateful.

Being the youngest of ten children, people often referred to me as "so and so's little sister." I think it was much easier for people to call me that rather than remember my name. Many of my siblings went off to college at Alabama A&M University and other schools, so when it was my time to go off to college, I chose to do something different. I went off to the

University of North Alabama (UNA) to chart my destiny.

Throughout my young adult years, I continued to go off the beaten path to position myself to find my identity. Though I strived to be different, I gleaned lessons from my siblings that have served me well in my personal and professional life.

I believe my experiences define me. Many of my qualities as CEO and founder of my company stem from those experiences. I have lived through all kinds of events and situations, and these were all influenced by the way I was brought up. I firmly believe that the way I dealt with having nine siblings brought me to where I am today! Somewhere along the way, I learned how to leverage my experiences and my siblings' characteristics to my advantage. This book was penned so that you can learn how to do the same.

The Power of Ten will help you build your leadership capabilities by understanding how to recognize characteristics in others that you can leverage to your personal and professional advantage. On the pages of this book, I will share a series of stories I have lived through and how I used them to arrive where I am today. My strength as a leader did not simply emerge from the ground -- my family, upbringing, and my amazing husband influenced the leader I have become.

THERE'S A LEADER IN YOU

So, what then is leadership? Indeed, if we are to discuss leadership, we must first establish its definition.

In general, leadership is defined as the ability to lead, influence, and guide others. Leadership is the ability to influence the behavior of other people by using persuasive communications. Leadership encompasses aspects of psychology, including emotional intelligence and social skills, among others. Good leadership also involves having a vision, setting priorities, motivating others, providing inspiration, communicating effectively, and overall, positively impacting others.

Every human being possesses the ability to lead. However, every human being does not recognize their ability to lead. In all transparency, I didn't always see myself as a leader. Before starting my company, I worked a 9-5. I started my company as a way to supplement my income. I began building my company over the weekends until the needs of PROJECTXYZ required my 9-5 attention. Naturally, I had to hire people because I couldn't be everywhere at once. One day, I looked up and realized that life's circumstances had forced me into becoming the leader I never saw hiding within myself.

Recognizing the power of leadership has allowed many to rise to great heights of success in their respective fields. They realized what I hope you will come to understand by the end of this book: Becoming a great leader is a matter of knowing your characteristics and skills and focusing on these as your advantages.

Within each of us lie great leadership qualities, even though we may have gaps that must be filled to attain our leadership goals. The purpose of this book is to help you recognize the leader within you and begin closing those gaps.

After reading the Power of Ten, I hope you will see the circumstances you face as propellers to your destiny as a leader. Finally, I hope you can see the leadership lessons surrounding you and allow them to shape you into the leader you desire to become.

Well, enough of the small talk! Let's get right to it.

One
ARE YOU SURE ABOUT THAT?

Leadership, in simple terms, is defined as influencing others to achieve a common set of goals and outcomes. Leaders are perceived as the supreme decision-makers in any given situation. As a leader, you are considered responsible for determining the operations process and what the team must do to accomplish its goals. Hence, part of leadership is being a dreamer capable of transferring what one believes is possible to those in place to help make it possible.

Dreams are a precious gift. I'm not referring to the dreams we have when we sleep or the fleeting ideas that leave our minds within a day. I'm speaking of the dreams we have when we are redesigning our lives around purpose. Those dreams stir our hearts and challenge our reality. Those dreams give volume to the internal, nagging, demanding voice that constantly asks leaders, "What if —?" and waits for an answer. Leader, what life do you imagine when you endeavor to ask yourself why you exist? How do you respond when you give your heart permission to dream? I often told my heart:

That's impossible.
You're never going to be able to make it happen. It's not your turn yet.
It's never been done before.
You're not young enough.
You're too young.
You're not smart enough.
You're not good enough.
It's too risky!

These are called limiting beliefs. Limiting beliefs are assumptions that keep you from reaching your goal. Limiting beliefs are not based on logic or evidence. They aren't valid, and deep down inside, you know it. However, it doesn't matter. Once these limiting beliefs make their way from your brain to your heart, you doubt yourself and question every dream you've ever had. If you dare to achieve the goals you have set, you must correct these limiting beliefs about yourself.

Limiting beliefs are different from the voice of reason. Limiting beliefs halt your dreams and restrain you from exploring the possibility of seeing them manifest. However, the voice of reason logically shows you the barriers, obstacles, and challenges that you must consider on the path to accomplishing your dreams. In this chapter, we will discuss the difference between limiting beliefs and the voice of reason in hopes that you will learn to recognize the two.

THE OPPORTUNITY: ELIMINATE LIMITING BELIEFS & LISTEN TO THE VOICE OF REASON

If you want to get to where you desire to go, you must have self-confidence. You must be confident in your abilities and refuse to allow limiting beliefs to hold you back. Our confidence is rooted in what we believe about ourselves. It is impossible to have positive self-confidence with a negative self-belief system. The journey to self-confidence begins by eliminating the limiting beliefs lurking in your mind. If you want to achieve anything in life, you must firmly believe that you are capable of doing so.

Unfortunately, limiting beliefs are the primary reason for much of what goes on in this world. These beliefs are so ingrained in our belief system that it is hard to separate them from reality. They are such a common part of our thought process that we imagine they are normal and legitimate. When we cannot recognize limiting beliefs as the true culprit of our unaccomplished goals, they continue to hold us back from reaching our true potential. After all, how can we eradicate something we don't know is there?

ELIMINATING LIMITING BELIEFS

With a strong, positive self-belief system, you can achieve everything you desire. The more confident you are, the more chances and success will come your way. Whatever you put out comes back to you — so if you see the best in people and think highly of yourself, you will draw people and circumstances into your life that will help you achieve your goals. Leaders who are happy and prosperous hang out with other happy leaders. Consider this. When you have limiting beliefs about yourself, you spend a lot of time second-guessing your abilities. You don't feel confident around other leaders. At a networking event, you spend more time wondering how you even got in the room than taking advantage of the connections in the room. You're probably not coherent, concentrated, or linked. Instead of making eye contact and starting up a wonderful conversation that could change your life, you could be staring at the carpet, worrying.

Limiting beliefs don't have to remain hidden in the fabric of your mind. Begin the process of eliminating them by first identifying them. For example, what do you tell yourself when you dream? Do your thoughts cause you to explore the possibility? Or, do they restrain you from even attempting to make it happen? What do you say to yourself that you would never say to a hopeful friend? The answers to these questions will help you uncover the limiting beliefs keeping you from accomplishing your dreams.

Once you identify these limiting beliefs, it is crucial to replace them with positivity. Each time you default to a limiting belief, you must intentionally redirect your thoughts and self-talk. As you practice this method regularly, you will notice that your limiting beliefs are fading away. It may take some time, but if you are consistent, your perspective and life will change completely.

LISTENING TO YOUR VOICE OF REASON

My sister, Flo, is my oldest sibling. Since I can remember, she has been the nurturer in our family – an attribute she undoubtedly acquired from our mom. Even before our mother became ill, Flo always took care of things for us. I have always looked up to my significantly older siblings and held them in high regard, dare I say, as idols. Not only was Flo the nurturer in the family, but she also served as the "voice of reason" we often didn't realize we needed. The official definition of the voice of reason is the person who tries to get everyone to make decisions using evidence and logic. For my family, Flo is like the little person sitting on our shoulders, helping us contemplate difficult decisions. She is always quick to provide a dose of reality with a side of compassion and care.

When I wanted to start my business, Flo had many concerns. I was a single parent at the time with a full-time job and benefits. Flo's concern came from a place of love and support. She pointed out things that could interfere with what I thought my future would be. She revealed the danger of leaving a job with benefits to chart off into entrepreneurship's unknown (and often murky) waters. Flo made it clear that as a single mother, I had a child who depended on me for survival. Leaving a solid job to do something I'd never done before could impact my ability to provide for my child. From my vantage point, starting a business would secure our future. However, Flo wanted me to be realistic about my circumstances and the impact my decision could have on my future. It was a classic case of risk versus uncertainty. Unfortunately, most of us don't know the difference between risk and uncertainty. Risk is the uncertain outcome of KNOWN future events or "the known unknown." Uncertainty, instead, is the uncertain outcome of UNKNOWN future events, or "the unknown unknown." The voice of reason helps you to explore risks. In contrast, limiting beliefs leaves you floating in uncertainty.

In her nurturing way, Flo was not trying to discourage me, and her comments certainly didn't come from a bad place; she just wanted me to be realistic. I knew Flo would support me in whatever I did, and that's the most comforting part. As you know by now, I went forth with my dream of leaving my 9-5 and establishing PROJECTXYZ. Instead of being upset with me for doing what I wanted to do, Flo helped me think everything through. She helped me explore the risks and uncover uncertainties. This is the power of the voice of reason.

Sometimes, as leaders, limiting beliefs and the voice of reason from within can sound the same. This is why you need someone in your life who can serve as your voice of reason when you have difficult, life-changing decisions to make. I am certainly grateful I have my sister, Flo. The voice of reason will give advice to support your options so that you can make a decision based on facts rather than emotional thinking.

You must be willing to listen in order to reap the benefits of having a voice of reason. I could have most certainly ignored Flo and gone through with what I thought was the best thing to do. However, because I listened to her concerns, I could glean from her wisdom and properly plan and prepare to achieve my dreams.

THE TAKEAWAY: LEARN HOW TO LISTEN

As a leader, it can be easy to fall into the trap of believing that you don't have to listen to others. When the final decision, impacts of risk, and pressure of navigation rests on your shoulder, you can feel like you don't need to listen to others. After all, you will be responsible for everything that happens after decisions are made. Though it may be a passive process, listening to others leads to active improvements. We must never underestimate the value of listening to those we lead and those who support us. It almost always ensures our success.

Listening allows leaders to gather enough important information so they can make sound decisions. The best decisions are based on data and not guesses, and feedback is one of the best ways to gather the data you need to make decisions. This is true for businesses, organizations, teams, etc. In every facet you may lead, feedback is vital to success.

Listening has several advantages. It improves efficiency, builds morale, decreases mistakes, makes you more famous, enhances your brand, and widens your network of relationships. Here are a few ways you can improve your listening skills as a leader:

Stop hearing and start listening instead.

Listening is not the same as hearing. When you are only partly participating in a discussion because you already have an agenda in mind and are waiting for the opportunity to express yourself, you aren't listening. You are only hearing. Listening requires you to lean into the individual speaking and attempt to understand, create trust, and empathize before forming ideas and suggestions. Active listening makes you influential.

To actively listen, you must place your phone on mute, tune out the background noise, tune in to the speaker, and concentrate on them. This extends to both your personal and professional lives.

Maintain direct eye contact.

Let's say you're conversing with someone at a business event when you notice someone else you want to chat with across the room. You break eye contact with the person in front of you, and your focus becomes making your way across the room. Not only are you no longer listening, but you've also made the person you're conversing with feel insignificant. Maintaining eye contact lets others know that you are listening and invested in what they are saying.

Consider what you've heard.

Mirroring (repeating back) or paraphrasing what the other person says will help you make sure you've heard it right and give the other person a chance to clear up any misunderstandings. People want to know that they've been noticed and that they've been understood.

Make inquiries.

One of the greatest ways to let others know that you are listening is by asking questions about what they say. In addition to showing attentiveness, this also communicates that you are invested in their advice and suggestions.

Anytime your dreams require you to make difficult decisions, you will be confronted by limiting beliefs and the voice of reason. Your ability to discern the difference between the two will be the determining factor of your success. Eliminate limiting beliefs by concentrating on the future and visualizing the ideal situation. It's all too tempting to get frustrated when you realize how far you must go, especially when setbacks are unavoidable. This is why it's important to keep your eyes forward and imagine your goals every day. Your dreams are unlikely to come true overnight. Your subconscious knows what to step toward if you look ahead and can see your dream in your mind before it happens. Imagine stunning possibilities emerging in front of you as you focus forward. Consider how wonderful it feels to be living your ideal life. Allow yourself to enjoy this sensation and the desire for what you want. You will become more receptive to receiving goodness, and your dreams will begin to manifest more easily.

On your journey to making your dreams a reality, welcome the wisdom, criticism, and critique of your voice of reason. Imagine a room, dark and vast, where any sound would reverberate back around you like a wave. It might feel like a chamber that has loads of echo, right? But an echo chamber does not need to be an actual physical structure. In real terms, an echo chamber can occur anywhere information is shared, whether online or face-to-face. Ultimately, when we don't listen to others, we miss the opportunity to hear information that could push us further and encourage our development. So don't just surround yourself with people who agree with you– don't stick yourself into an echo chamber. Instead, welcome the voice of reason.

As leaders, we understand the power of listening and practice good listening skills to gain the data we need to make the best decisions. However, we also understand the difference between voices of reason and those of negativity. The goal of negative people is to minimize the big dreams of ambitious people. They will warn you that you are wasting your time or that there will be no jobs available. It's the same old story. People have been stifling their potential because they lack confidence in themselves. Ignore them! If you believe in your heart that your dream is achievable and you want to pursue it, you CAN have it. Remember that the world is filled with infinite resources that are accessible to all. Those who believe so strongly in their dream that they can sense it before it becomes physical will never be without the resources they need to succeed. This is a key principle in the Law of Attraction. So don't give up on your dream, and don't listen to those who say it can't be done. Hundreds of thousands of stories exist of people thriving and achieving their goals, seemingly against all odds. These are the people you should be paying attention to.

On the other hand, you want guidance, encouragement, and assistance from people you respect who are strong and optimistic. Surround yourself with those who believe in the power of positivity, such as colleagues, mentors, and teachers. You are the number of the people with whom you associate. So choose people who have confidence in you and themselves. Find wise advice and guidance from those who have already achieved success, and make friends with those who are obviously on their way. You'll know because they enjoy pursuing their dreams and ambitions! They are motivated to get up and work for their goals. They encourage you and pay attention to your plans. They just have constructive criticism and will always tell you that you should do it! It's difficult to say goodbye to old friends, but if you're moving in a new direction and want to be the best you can be, you'll naturally begin to make new friends who share your values, dreams, and optimistic outlook.

Finally, take the risks you feel are appropriate! There will be moments when you are at a loss about what to do. To step ahead, you sometimes have to take a huge risk. For example, you may need to relocate to a new city and leave your old life behind, or you may need to embark on a business venture that will make or break you. There will be risks along the way, but only those that feel good should be taken. The risks that will lead you down the right path will feel special. Everything about it would make you feel better. Your heart will compel you to take action and say, "Yes!" You will feel lighter, and if you imagine your future, it'll be entirely optimistic and look and feel good. If your intuition gives you contradictory signals or your imagination leads you down a negative road, this may not be the path for you. However, if an opportunity feels good to you and comes from a good place with good people, take it, even if it's risky, because it might be the next logical step toward your dream life!

Two

DO WE HAVE A PROBLEM?

Whenever something major happened in our home, my siblings and I would look to Maceo for guidance to solve a problem. We all figured that if dad didn't know the answer, Maceo certainly did – on the rare occasion that he didn't, he would certainly find out.

Maceo has always done his own thing. Once he went away to college, he never came home. He lived in Atlanta, and as a child, I visited him every summer and spring break. Visiting Maceo was my get-away. Back then, the city seemed larger than life. Atlanta was our New York. There was so much to do and see, and I wanted to do and see it all. I just loved it!

Having a big brother who lived in a fast-paced city was a pretty big deal to me. Maceo would take me to Six Flags, Centennial Olympic Park, and every place in between. I would visit the massive buildings he worked in and often stood in awe of all he had become. I imagined my big brother had to be smart to compete in an environment like Atlanta effectively.

Maceo and his wife didn't have children. They always made me feel welcome at their home and cared for me as if I were their child. I felt extremely close to them. When my mother became ill, they invited me to live with them. My parents never agreed to it. So, I stayed home, and my other siblings and I took care of each other.

I was and always will be grateful for the support they afforded me. Their home was a safe place I could visit to figure things out. When I got divorced, my daughter and I moved to Atlanta and lived with Maceo and his wife for six months. After years of visiting as a child, as an adult, I still went to my safe place for healing. I knew my big brother would have my back.

Maceo was a genius in my eyes, and I always viewed him as a "whiz kid." Even though he worked in corporate America, he always had a side hustle, and I admired that about him. He was smart enough to know that anything could happen when working for someone else, so he made sure he had a backup plan. Having worked for several Fortune 500 companies, he was a valuable asset when I decided to start my business. I called on him to help me with my first business plan and contract template. I wanted to soak up every ounce of knowledge he had about running a business.

One thing I gleaned from Maceo was the ability to keep a leveled head and make wise decisions to solve difficult problems. For leaders in any capacity, this is an invaluable lesson. It goes without saying that Maceo's success is attributed to his strong problem-solving skills. Without question, working for Fortune 500 companies and his side hustles presented challenges daily. I imagine that my brother was often faced with the choice to (1) be irrational and allow the stress of the problems he faced to overwhelm him or (2) choose to rise above the challenge and find a solution. His success is tangible evidence of his decision to do the latter.

THE OPPORTUNITY: DEVELOP EMOTIONAL INTELLIGENCE

Problem-solving is an unavoidable part of life, especially for leaders. Life is filled with twists and turns, starts and stops, requiring us to solve issues every step of the way. I find it fascinating and somewhat baffling that by the time many have reached adulthood, they have not mastered the art of problem-solving. Lacking mastery of these areas is a major leadership gap for many individuals who have the potential to be great leaders.

Great leaders are great problem solvers. Great problem solvers are great thinkers. These individuals have less drama and problems to begin with and don't get overly emotional when faced with difficulty. They usually see problems as challenges and life experiences and try to stand above them objectively. These great leaders typically have high EQ or emotional intelligence.

The term emotional intelligence is widely used these days. It is a concept about how an individual learns to deal with life and others. Individuals with a high EQ tend to be more creative and resourceful in their dealings with other people. Emotionally intelligent people are perceived to be more successful in their social interactions and professional lives because of their ability to put things into perspective.

Emotional intelligence comprises facets of self-awareness, self-regulation, motivation, and empathy. These four aspects are essential when assessing one's emotions or how one deals with other people and events. The better one is with self-awareness, self-regulation, motivation, and empathy, the more developed their emotional intelligence.

Many leaders shy away from developing their emotional intelligence because it requires them to become aware of unpleasant emotions as they creep into their consciousness through feelings and moods. Developing emotional intelligence demands us to be more intentional about pausing to explore emotions before we react to them and anticipating the impact certain emotions have on us. Though it can be a daunting task, once mastered, we can respond to our emotions differently and stop them from negatively influencing our actions. Like with any skill, the more we practice emotional intelligence, the more instinctive it becomes.

You've probably figured this out by now, but it is impossible to master emotional intelligence without mastering self-awareness. Leaders who have mastered self-awareness know how they impact those they lead because they are aware of how they impact themselves. They are aware of their behaviors and the impact their emotions have on their thought processes, performance, decision-making, and problem-solving. Being self-aware allows leaders to change their behavior in the face of conflict or when required to implement certain changes. It also helps them avoid unhealthy behavior that they may have in front of other people. Therefore, if you want to close gaps in your leadership abilities, become aware of yourself. Study your skills, strengths, and weaknesses and how they positively or negatively impact you and others.

Much of the fear and anxiety leaders face when making decisions or searching for solutions can be resolved by developing their emotional intelligence. Mastering our emotional intelligence increases our ability to better manage and understand our fears and anxiety. Once we master emotional intelligence, we're better able to work with these feelings rather than against them and act more intuitively. As the management of our emotions improves, so does our intuition. Intuition is a potent source of information. When we can trust our gut instinct, we can make decisions and act faster.

Great leaders use a combination of intuition and logic to solve problems and make decisions. They are reasonably open-minded but logically skeptical. Intuition has more to do with our emotional and intuitive side, and logic is more related to our cognition and thinking. Great leaders use both of these forces to get as much information as possible to come up with the best possible solution or the wisest decision.

Resilience

If you were to ask any leader who has achieved any level of success to transparently share about their journey, you are sure to hear about the ups and downs and challenges they faced along the way. Within moments, you will recognize that their resilience played a major part in their success. Great leaders must be resilient, especially when solving problems because even the greatest solutions produce hurdles. Leaders who don't possess resilience throw in the towel after several attempts. However, great leaders don't stop at the first, second, or even third hurdle. They believe in what they are producing and stop at nothing to resolve issues that get in the way of production!

Resilience is about being able to bounce back after setbacks, disappointments, and struggles, and it is one of our most powerful personal indicators of succeeding in any task. By definition, resilience is an enduring quality that permits you to deal with obstacles. By being resilient and persistent, great leaders find positive outcomes in whatever circumstances arise. When faced with adversity, we have several options to manage the challenge. We can cope with it. We can recover from it. We can bounce back. We can fight it. Or, we can succumb to it. We all admire leaders who respond to adversity with dignity, strength, resiliency, grace, and creativity. We are amazed at their ability to think rationally and face problems head-first instead of letting themselves react to them irrationally and emotionally. While emotion is important, it shouldn't hold one back from

TWO: DO WE HAVE A PROBLEM?

reaching their potential. The resilient leaders we hold in high regard understand this, and if we are to close gaps in our leadership, we must glean from their diligence.

Resilience is a state of being able to adapt, not just physically but also mentally and emotionally. As I explained in the introduction, we are all shaped by our life experiences. Resilience is a state of mind that is shaped by experiences that humans go through in their lives. It's a state of mind that we all possess and all of us need. If you lack resilience, you may struggle to have the strength of character required to rise above challenges and survive the ups and downs of life without taking a very long time to recover. Thus, resilience is a major part of any leadership journey.

Being resilient requires conscious control over how you deal with both negative and positive emotions. Self-care is vital for maintaining resilience. Self-care is more than just about treating yourself to a spa day or a nice lunch. It's also about carving out time to be creative, venting negative emotions, learning how to manage conflict, spending time with loved ones, implementing change that is conducive to the life we desire, eating healthy, developing self-esteem and assertiveness, developing and improving your self-belief skills, and creating meaningful relationships. In short, if you want to be resilient, you need to self-care. This doesn't mean that you'll never have a setback, but it does mean that you can rise above the setbacks that life offers you.

The Takeaway: Embrace Problems!

As leaders, we face complex obstacles that can seem insurmountable at times. I'm referring to the type of issues that can keep you up at night, cause you to drink a third (or fourth) cup of coffee, and leave you tired and irritated. Even though you may feel like you will never come up with the right solutions, don't be discouraged. There are tactics you can use to reposition and refresh your mindset. You have the ability to come up with innovative solutions to the most challenging leadership issues. Often what you need is a new insight to come up with the next brilliant idea. Here are a few tactics you can try when you are faced with the opportunity to problem solve!

Determine the source of the problem.

When confronted with a problem, there are often a number of complicating factors that make finding a solution difficult. Problems tend to pile up easily, and it's almost impossible to fix them all at once. Take some time to find the origin of the problem before attempting to solve it. Identifying the root cause of the problem, whether it's a faulty mechanism, a lack of instruction, or a communication failure, will help you solve the problem faster and better rather than spinning your wheels. If you are having trouble determining the source of the problem, start with the most serious issue and work your way down.

Dissect the procedure.

If the problem is a defective or inefficient method, take the time to map out what needs to be fixed or improved. There is no such thing as a minor move. Taking the time to plan out the process from beginning to end, whether using a list, flow chart, whiteboard, or even pen and paper, will help you imagine all of the steps. In addition, this will make it easier to spot where something isn't working properly.

Seek the advice of a new set of eyes.

Collaborating with others is one way to improve your problem-solving abilities. If you're stuck, it may be time to enlist the aid of a new set of eyes to help you solve the problem. After a while, you might become so engrossed in the issue that you begin to close your eyes. Consider it akin to true crime shows where the detective has tunnel vision on a single suspect. You can become so preoccupied with one question, concept, or solution that you restrict your brainstorming or become preoccupied with the problem at hand. Bringing in a partner who isn't already working on the issue might be just what you need to get your creative juices flowing again. They will serve as an objective sounding board, encouraging you to consider new ideas and approaches to the problem.

Failure isn't anything to be scared of.

Fear of failure can stifle our ability to solve problems. When you are afraid of failing, you may restrict your brainstorming and ideas. When trying out new ideas, there's always a chance they might fail, but it's better to investigate a risky idea rather than reject it outright. You should be able to minimize some (possibly even all) of the risk if you take the time to vet your proposals thoroughly. Attempting something you have never done before can be terrifying. However, the best inventions are always the result of overcoming fear of failure and attempting new, risky ideas.

Pause for a moment.

Do you have a dilemma that you can't solve? You may be familiar with the term "writer's block." It's the same thing, except instead of words, it's ideas that aren't flowing. Often, you will get stuck and won't come up with new ideas or solutions. It's all right! This is a perfectly normal phenomenon. According to studies, the brain can only concentrate on a task or mission for 52 minutes before being fatigued and blocked.

Take More Breaks!

To improve your problem-solving skills, make sure your brain can process data efficiently and easily before putting it to use. You deplete your brain's capacity to do good work when you are too tired, depressed, or burned out. Take breaks in the day to avoid these harmful consequences. Finding a way to incorporate breaks into your day, whether you use a phone timer or a computer app, will make you feel more refreshed and efficient when tackling big challenges.

Putting these suggestions into effect will help you come up with new ideas to solve problems. You can become more effective at finding innovative solutions to the toughest leadership problems by improving your problem-solving skills. Who knows, the next idea could be absolutely brilliant and spark something incredible!

Three
DID YOU SEE THAT?

More than anything else, there's one personality trait that is becoming increasingly valuable. It's a trait that allows some leaders to see critical patterns where others only see a random series of events. This trait enables leaders to recognize when something important is missing when others fail to notice. Lacking this trait can cause embarrassment, and as leaders. None of us can afford that, right? So, what is this indispensable trait? It's attention to detail! Every organization needs people who are conceptual and can see the "big picture." Still, if this is not balanced with people who pay the appropriate level of attention to detail, leaders may be setting their organizations up for disaster.

My sister Charlene is extraordinarily detail-oriented. She is an accounting executive and was my Chief Financial Officer (CFO) for many years. She is the first one that I remember still being in the house when I was growing up. She is fifteen years older than me, and she would always call me her hip baby because she carried me around and looked out for me when I was a child.

Ironically, Charlene's daughter and I share a birthday, and I often joke with my niece, telling her that she ruined my Sweet 16 birthday because my sister, who always looked after me, was having a baby of her own on my birthday! The nerve of her!

As my CFO, Charlene would always make sure that everything matched up to the penny, and that's a great attribute to have in someone responsible for reporting your books. I appreciate her and her "eagle-eye!"

THE OPPORTUNITY: PAY ATTENTION TO THE DETAILS

Most leadership conversations tend to place great emphasis is on the visionary components of being a great leader. However, it is also crucial for leaders to value the ability to see the details and invest in those around them who possess this skill. The details matter in everything, from sports to business, cooking to painting, engineering to medicine, ballroom dancing to stamp collecting, bicycle maintenance to playing the violin. It's not only important for the outcome of the task at hand, but it can also lead to success in nearly every area of life. One small detail can be the deciding factor between success and failure.

For example, in sports, the importance of detail goes far beyond the apparent results. You need skill, speed, endurance, strength, and knowledge of how each tiny detail in the play affects the game's outcome. Without those skills, winning would be much more difficult to achieve. You must possess the ability to think fast on your feet, use your skills to plan, and visualize every tiny detail. This minimizes the possibility of losing a game.

Each detail of anything we produce has its significance. When all the details come together to create a great result, they all make perfect sense. If the details aren't done perfectly, the end product may be a mess.

In the world of manufacturing or any industry for that matter, there are always areas of need for efficiency and cost reduction. While these things are often inevitable, they can be eliminated by making simple changes that most people aren't even aware of. For example, when a product goes out the door or is dropped off to be shipped to its destination, it's not only the item itself that has to be carefully packaged for shipping, but the process has to be detailed enough for you to be on top of your game and for your business to work well. It also has to have proper packaging so that the product doesn't break or, in the case of electronic items, have the possibility of becoming damaged during shipping. Each of these processes has details that can ruin the quality of your product and thus the customer experience. This is why attention to detail is key!

THE TAKEAWAY: DEVELOP SKILLS NECESSARY FOR THE DETAILS

So, how do we develop our ability to give attention to detail? Much like any valuable skill set, there are many components to learning to value the details. Let's discuss a few of them.

Organizational Skills

Can you sort through documents quickly and find what you need without feeling overwhelmed? Can you schedule tasks to be completed at specific times without feeling like you have too much on your plate? Are you able to stay focused on a task without interruption for another pressing task?

You would be amazed at how many leaders would answer "no" to those questions. It's rather difficult for leaders to pay attention to the details when their office, daily schedule, mind, home, and other aspects of their lives are unorganized. When things are 'all over the place,' you tend to spend a lot of time putting out fires because you weren't organized enough to manage issues before they became emergencies. So, naturally, leading in this manner doesn't allow the opportunity to see the details. If leaders are to become more detailed-oriented, they must begin with getting organized.

No matter where you lead, you have a lot of responsibilities and tasks to do. You need a good system to keep track of those tasks. Organizational skills allow you to create this system. Good examples of organization techniques are: using tools like calendars, day planners, highlighters, resource management software, project planning software, and any kind of apps and programs created to help you stay highly organized. Many of us tend not to use them, but they can help us stay organized. When we are organized, we can intentionally focus on tasks and give appropriate attention to every detail.

As leaders, another key component of organization we often overlook is creating clear descriptions of our organizations or projects. When you have a clear description of the overall purpose of what you do and how it benefits its beneficiaries, you can begin to have clear goals to work towards. Clear descriptions give you a starting point to create goals and a clear path toward reaching them. When you are clear on the goal and the path, you can better see the details necessary for success. Many organizations become unorganized and unfocused because leaders do not understand what they are trying to achieve and how they can achieve their goals. It's no wonder they miss out on the important details. You can't determine vital details when you are unclear on what you want to achieve. Leader, it's up to you to create a plan or delegate what you cannot do very well to individuals who can help you out.

One of the most important organizational skills is time management. With proper management skills, you can effectively plan and manage your time and the time of those who work with you on this project. You also increase the likelihood of completing projects in a time span that leads to better results. Ultimately, you cannot succeed if you cannot manage your time the right way.

Time Management Skills

Leaders with poor time management skills view giving attention to small details as time-consuming. Typically, it's because they haven't allotted the appropriate time to complete a task, whether due to overscheduling, unplanned distractions or hiccups, or redoing something that wasn't done correctly the first time around, and don't have the time necessary to focus on small details.

Time management skills are crucial for attention to detail skills. Excellent and effective time-management skills go hand-in-hand with good organizational abilities. Great time management skills include setting goals, prioritizing your goals, creating a schedule, making lists, and using different types of software such as time management tools, timekeeping software, and more.

In addition to ensuring you have time for the details, great time management skills help you achieve more in a given time. Having these skills will also help you reduce stress, increase productivity, and heighten success rates. Prioritization is a skill that has been a mainstay of business success since the beginning of time. Even our ancestors needed to know what to prioritize— food and water over leisure. The same applies to any success story, including your projects. Today, the process of prioritizing has become a new way of managing time. The importance of prioritizing is not only limited to time management. It also applies to solving problems, finding solutions, completing tasks, planning, and overall effectiveness. Hence, learn when to say no and focus on one task, as certain milestones cannot be achieved if you aren't prioritizing tasks that need to be done beforehand.

Another essential tool in time management is timing, the ability to set a suitable schedule for any given activity at a particular time and date. You do not need to stick with the same scheduled activity every day or even on some days. In fact, you can rearrange the scheduled activities so that they are more effective in meeting the pressing needs of the current situation. Nonetheless, you need to know when to time specific tasks and achievements to achieve the goals set. Planning when you will take care of certain tasks or activities will position you to schedule enough time to pay attention to the details.

Analytical Thinking Skills

Analytical thinking skills allow you to gather and analyze information, look at issues or ideas through different points of view, and solve problems. If you desire to become more focused and concentrated, strive to improve your analytical skills. When it comes to paying attention to details, analytical skills aid you in determining what details are essential. Since they play a major role in our decision-making process, having great analytical skills will allow you to pinpoint the critical details and set aside the appropriate amount of time needed to execute them.

Analytical skills refer to the ability to gather and analyze data and arrive at solutions to problems. These skills are essential for leaders in any organization, both small and large. Individuals with strong analytical skills can solve problems and improve an organization's overall success and productivity.

Analytical skills aren't all about numbers and data. In fact, they lead to a greater understanding of human nature and psychology, which enables people to make better decisions based on real-world experiences. Such skills are important for leaders to achieve success, as they lead one to better understand why certain reactions are occurring and why people exhibit certain behaviors. Therefore, with these skills, leaders become more apt to see where problems occur and hence solve them early on. You do not have to be good at mathematics or science to develop analytical skills; you simpy need to analyze data and determine relevant information—this isn't as technical as it sounds!

Observation Skills

Finally, we will discuss the most prominent skill necessary when improving our attention to detail: OBSERVATION SKILLS. Leaders who possess strong observation skills can quickly pinpoint and prioritize what is important in any particular moment. Some leaders are very observant by nature; many are not.

There are many easy ways and tools to improve your keen sense of observation. These include practicing mindfulness, slowing down to "smell the roses," meditation, asking intentional questions, and being a more active listener. Each of these actions requires you to quiet your mind and focus on the moment or project at hand.

Many leaders have poor observation skills because they are always on the go, have a million things running through their minds at once, or are focused on the next big thing. Suppose you want to improve your ability to pay attention to the details. Practice slowing down and allowing yourself to observe your surroundings. Of all the skills, this one is the most important for leaders. When embarking upon a new leadership role, it is not always easy to know what people are thinking or doing when you first encounter them. You may need more experience to gain a better understanding of the organization or business. It takes some practice to develop observation skills, but once you get the hang of it, you will effortlessly learn about those around you and vital details.

I'm not sure if you caught it, but most of these skills work hand-in-hand. As you work diligently to improve your attention to detail skills, it may be challenging to know where to start. Wherever you choose to begin, remember to take it one step at a time. Rome wasn't built in a day, and your ability to see the details won't likely improve overnight. However, as with any skill, you can achieve this necessary skill set with repetition and intentionality. Your organization and those you lead will benefit significantly from your decision to see the details.

Four
THE BOLD & THE BEAUTIFUL

Boldness is fundamentally about confidence and courage. Bold leaders come in all shapes, sizes, ages, backgrounds, and cultures. Bold leaders are clear about what they want and where they are headed in life. Each day, they say "yes" to their future and surrender to the growth opportunities that surface along their journey. Bold leaders aren't naive to challenges and setbacks; they expect and embrace them. Most importantly, bold leaders are not afraid to stand up for their beliefs.

There are many leaders whom I admire for their strength and grace. When things go wrong, as it often does, they HANDLE it. They handle it in a thousand different ways on a thousand different days, but they do so boldly, even as they make time to care for and nurture others.

It's worth clarifying that boldness is not about how outgoing you are, an introvert can be just as bold as an extrovert, and you may well be bold in some areas of your life and not in others. Boldness is much more about having the courage to be true to yourself.

Courage helps us overcome our weaknesses, keeping us moving toward our goals. When we are willing to do what is right, even when we are afraid of the consequences, we move into a new world where we see that anything is possible. This is where true lasting success begins. You can achieve your goals even if you think you will face all kinds of challenges that are hard to overcome. You need to understand that you've got the ability to do whatever it takes -- no matter what. Even if you feel like you don't have the potential, you still have the opportunity to make things happen if you are courageous enough to take the first step.

So, why is boldness important for success? First, it allows leaders to push themselves hard, which is vital for leading anything and being successful at it!

My sister Mary is definitely bold and beautiful. She is tall, slender, and what many men would call attractive. Growing up, if I had to jump sharp or get dressed up for something, I would always go to Mary and borrow something from her closet. Mary is bold, daring, and fearlessly goes for what she wants. When we were growing up, there wasn't a "name" for someone like Mary. Now, I guess she would be characterized as a strong, black woman! Mary has three kids, and she had her first child when she was still in high school. As you can imagine, many people tried to put a "scarlet letter" on her, but Mary stayed true to herself. She was still very popular and was elected homecoming queen, even though the teachers didn't want her to have the title because they felt that someone who had a baby out of wedlock shouldn't represent the school as homecoming queen. Do you think Mary let that stop her? Absolutely not. My sister was and still is one tough cookie.

Mary has also been married and divorced, but she never let what some people may perceive as failures get her down. As I said, she is that sibling who always goes after what she desires. Mary has the innate ability to see her circumstances as growth opportunities. She understood that the only reason to be ashamed of failure is to learn from the experience.

Mary taught me that no matter what life throws at you, you have to keep going. You can't let situations, failures, circumstances, and the like stop you from being authentically you. Challenges are the spice of life. Some challenges are easier to overcome than others, as many may have a lasting effect on an individual. However, if we persevere, we will overcome every obstacle we face. When we look at life through this perspective, we see hope, and as a leader, you must adopt this mindset to achieve true success and operate in boldness.

Take note that we are discussing courage rather than being free of fear. The truth is, fear is something we cannot fully live without. It tells us when danger is around or when we need to be aware of the risks. We can't get rid of fear, but we can build the courage to overcome it one challenge at a time.

THE OPPORTUNITY: UNLOCK YOUR BOLDNESS

What comes to your mind when you think of a bold leader? You may immediately envision someone you admire. They are probably someone who is quickly recognized, exudes accomplishment, and exudes happiness. They exemplify what it means to be self-assured. What makes them so self-assured? What must you do to view yourself in the same light? As with most characteristics, there are some behaviors of bold leaders you can incorporate into your life to increase your boldness, and as a result, heighten your chances to succeed! Let's discuss a few habits and behaviors of bold leaders.

Bold leaders question the 'norm.'

Rarely do you come across a self-assured leader who simply goes with the flow, never challenging what they are told or raising an eyebrow at the 'norm.' Additionally, you will never find a bold leader who is surprisingly ordinary.

I'm not talking about the leaders who forcibly interject their commentary about everything or those who find peace in letting life unfold in the 'flow.' Rather, I'm referring to the leaders who rarely miss the opportunity to ask, "Why?" They ask questions like, "Why are things carried out that way? Could there possibly be an easier way to do things?"

Bold leaders aren't afraid to say, "Actually, no, that doesn't work for me," or "Let's try it this way." Furthermore, bold leaders are never embarrassed to say, "Okay, that didn't work. Let's try something new again."

Bold leaders only say yes when they mean it.

Some leaders say yes to everything. They don't want to disappoint others, and one of their biggest fears is letting someone down. Sadly, these leaders end up doing more for others than they ever do for themselves. Sound like anyone you know? *Possibly you?*

Many people find it difficult to utter the word "no," because it is a straightforward and conclusive response. 'No' is a strong term that can be hurtful when used wrongly. It can also be an abrupt end to any conversation. However, a self-assured leader understands that saying "no" to others is sometimes the only way to say "yes" to self.

As a leader, make your 'yes' count. Before you say it, understand the sacrifice it will require, and don't say 'yes' half-heartedly. The more you practice this, the more your 'yes' will mean to others.

Bold leaders use positive words in conversation.

One of my business mentors once told me how vital our words are. His example included simple words that we use in our daily conversations. He clarified that instead of saying, "Don't forget," we should say, "Please remember." Positive words are much more likely to elicit a response than negative ones.

In their interactions, confident leaders use encouraging words to uplift themselves and others. Bold leaders know they don't have to bring other people down to be happy. Individuals are motivated after conversing with confident leaders.

Bold leaders have a clear set of objectives and a strategy for achieving them.

A self-assured leader recognizes that while goals are significant, goals are meaningless if not accompanied by strategy. Until you have developed a strategy to achieve them, your goals and targets are nothing more than dreams. Bold leaders are familiar with setting goals, action plans, and strategies. Their success is attributed to their ability to make intentional shots at their targets.

Bold leaders understand that confidence goes beyond appearance, but they never underestimate the value of their "power outfit."

Everyone has at least one outfit or piece of clothing that makes them feel energetic, secure, and capable of taking on the world -- their outfit of power. Although confidence is based on far more than attire, bold leaders recognize that any small boost of confidence, even if it comes from a perfectly fitted blazer or a pair of killer heels, is well worth it.

Bold leaders exhibit self-assured body language.

Think Wonder Woman and Superman...but with more comfortable-fitting clothing. In their movie promotions, Wonder Woman and Superman strike poses that are confident and powerful. Without knowing what the movie is about, movie watchers are instantly drawn in and intrigued. The advantages of the power pose are based on a lot of psychology, and bold leaders know how to use it to their advantage. Even if they aren't feeling very optimistic on any given day, bold leaders know that with a power pose, they can fake it until they make it. Furthermore, you'll seldom see bold leaders hunched over or cowering in a crowd. Since these leaders believe in themselves, they stand tall, keep direct eye contact, and smile.

Bold leaders are aware of their personality traits, including their strengths and weaknesses.

Understanding yourself can be crucial to your success. A self-assured leader recognizes their strengths and limitations and knows how to exploit them. Bold leaders understand what it takes to be effective during the day and commit to their morning routine. They refuse to start working until they have had time to drink their coffee, do their meditation, and respond to emails. Bold leaders recognize what they do well and implement strategies or staff individuals to cover areas of weakness. That is why they are such successful leaders.

Bold leaders don't need to destroy others to achieve success.

A bold leader would never say, "Well, I did that better than you." Instead, bold leaders understand that their success has nothing to do with the shortcomings of others. Bold leaders own their achievements. They work hard to accomplish them and recognize that others' achievements are similar. Bold leaders avoid the trap of comparison at all costs. They are happy to assist and celebrate others' accomplishments.

Bold leaders concentrate on the positive and ignore

negative behaviors (and people).

Being in the company of a self-assured leader is like injecting a huge dose of positivity into your day. A bold leader has little time for the world's Negative Nellies and eliminates them from their life. They possess the amazing ability to see the bright side of any situation and leave you feeling motivated.

Like everyone else, bold leaders have bad days. They can't be 100 percent optimistic all of the time because that's unlikely. Nevertheless, they try to see the good in the world and surround themselves with positivity. To embrace your boldness, you don't have to be fake-optimistic (no one wants that)—all it takes is a slight change in perspective to see the silver lining and see the lesson in any setback.

Bold leaders recognize the value of self-care.

A self-assured leader understands that the first person they must look after is self. And, if they can't look after themselves, they won't be able to look after anyone else. Bold leaders make time for self-care regularly, even if it means waking up half an hour earlier just to sit and drink their coffee while it's still hot. Bold leaders understand that self-care is essential to success. A self-assured leader understands that grinding to a halt to achieve success is not a viable option. Bold leaders communicate when they need support or a break, even though they may not like it.

Bold leaders take risks and step outside of their comfort zone.

Stepping outside of your comfort zone, whether you're an extrovert, an introvert, or anywhere in between, can be difficult. On the other hand, an optimistic leader understands that nothing great has ever been accomplished in comfort. A confident leader is okay with getting outside their comfort zone every now and then, even though it takes some time and effort. They also recommend it. Bold leaders understand that the only way they will develop is to push themselves, and they are confident in their ability to do so.

THE TAKEAWAY: TRUE BOLDNESS COMES FROM WITHIN

While there are many awesome ways to unlock your boldness, you must begin with having positive inner beliefs about yourself. (Remember when we discussed limiting beliefs in chapter one?) In addition to acting bold, you must believe that you are bold, amazing, and powerful!

It's time to do some introspection. Examine yourself and give yourself credit for everything you accomplish—and even everything you try to accomplish. Allow yourself to make mistakes, grow from them, and learn from them. Be precisely who you are right now, not who you might be or who you think you should be. Embrace your individuality!

Recognize that self-assurance comes from within. Confidence is the belief that you have the capacity, ambition, and willpower to accomplish "X." (whatever it is you love to do, do well, and kick butt at). Nobody can take away your self-assurance because it is dependent on who you are. No one can take your courage or willpower away from you.

Nobody else has the power to take away your right to pursue your dreams. This is something you make for yourself from the inside.

You are fantastic. I believe in you, and I know you're a badass! It can be difficult to connect with your inner Beyoncé, Jay-Z, or whatever celeb-with-confidence floats your boat. For many, people have always tried to humble you or convince you that you should be quieter or less daring. For years, you were convinced that it was always better to always put the needs of others before your own. As a result, you've lost sight of how awesome you are.

You've probably been worried that if you walk around a powerful, confident woman, you'll come off as a witch with a capital 'B.' Maybe, you've been concerned that if you walk with your head held high, you'll come off as a cold, heartless man. Understand that there is a difference between boldness and arrogance, and there is absolutely nothing wrong with being a self-assured, positive, and bold leader.

Decide today to embrace your self-assurance and be the dynamic, entertaining, kickass leader you have always desired to be. Tell yourself that you are wonderful, fantastic, amazing, and hot because you are, leader!

Five
Oh, I See You Got Jokes!

My brother, Maurice, is always ready to tell a joke. Though he is quite the comedian, you have to listen closely. More often than not, his jokes always include words of wisdom. You never know when he is serious or possibly joking, so you always have to pay close attention. At one moment, he could be giving great information, and the very next, he is making a joke. I liken it to that character "Two-Face" in the Batman comics played by Harvey Dent. Of course, Maurice isn't a villain like this character, but he can discern which "face" is appropriate in a given situation. As a result, people warm up to him quickly, and he usually has excellent work relationships.

Maurice taught me how to be more light-hearted as a leader. In the world of leadership, some people take themselves far too seriously. Don't get me wrong, some instances require intense focus, and we should not take them light-heartedly. However, every moment in leadership does not require a grim face. Powerful leaders know the difference and use laughter to climb the ladder of success.

THE OPPORTUNITY: USE HUMOR AS A KEY TO SUCCESS!

Humor is humanity's greatest gift. It's the essence of creation. People enjoy following and working with leaders they like. For instance, employees spend chunks of their waking hours in the office. They may not say it, but they don't want their work to feel like a death march. Employees thrive better in healthily humorous environments. Humor is a potent stress buster. It offers a cognitive shift in how you view your stressors and a physical response that relaxes you when you laugh. Since humor also boosts morale, work environments that welcome humor have high retention and low turnovers. Leaders who know when to use humor in the office more than likely have employees who enjoy coming to work, despite how strenuous the labor may be.

As a leader, when you know how to use humor effectively, people will enjoy working and serving with you, as it is a great way to win friends and influence people. Humor is humanizing, and it allows leaders to find common ground with those they lead. It closes status gaps among leaders and employees/volunteers, and as a result, allows leaders to address serious concerns without causing employees/volunteers anxiety or fear. A tasteful joke has the ability to break tension, nervousness and put others at ease.

Sometimes, cracking a joke with a new acquaintance is all that is needed to break the ice and develop an organic connection because humor helps build trust. You can build trust with effective humor because it often reveals the authentic person lurking under the professional mask. Humor allows others to distinguish your true self from your professional self easily. As a result, others will believe you have nothing to hide. Leaders who use humor appear honest and have a childlike quality about them that draws others in. Authenticity and trust go a long way in leadership.

Humor doesn't just help leaders connect with others; it is also a key ingredient in creative thinking. For example, leaders who laugh in response to a conflict tend to shift from convergent thinking, where they can see only one solution, to divergent thinking, where multiple ideas are considered. Humor helps leaders play with ideas, lower their internal critique, and see things in new ways. It allows them to see challenges in novel ways and make connections they never considered.

With all of these amazing benefits, it's surprising that many leaders don't encourage healthy laughter. In fact, some prefer stern and strict work environments. You may be one of them. Some leaders believe that to appear hardworking, they can't enjoy laughter among those they lead. The truth is, we all tend to take ourselves too seriously. People won't dismiss you as a leader if you welcome healthy comedic relief now and then. Ironically, it is leaders who are too serious that people rarely take seriously.

By nature, humor is edgy. In professional environments where you are expected to wear a 9-5 or business mask, laughter can seem inappropriate. More often than not, leaders who feel like they can't share a laugh with those they lead have negative inner beliefs about themselves that keep them from showing glimpses of their humanity. They more than likely battle with perfectionism or creating healthy boundaries. For these leaders, humor is risky; their imperfections could be revealed, or people may begin to feel too "at home" with them and lose respect. However, successful leaders know that it's easier to connect with people on common ground. They have also mastered the art of sharing a laugh and maintaining productive expectations and boundaries with those they lead. They are secure in themselves, so they don't go overboard with jokes to be accepted. They understand how to leverage a laugh amongst employees or volunteers.

In most organizations and work environments, there is an unseen line between leaders and those being led. As a result, many people avoid humor to impress leaders that appear reserved, even if it causes them to hide their true selves. As a result, most jovial people claim to be reserved to appease their superiors. If the environments in which you lead seem stiff and tense, consider your personality. Is it possible that you have stifled laughter in your organization or office space? Additionally, because everyone has a different sense of humor, some people may hold back to avoid being labeled as someone with a poor sense of humor.

As a leader, allowing healthy humor into the spaces you lead is key to your success and the organization's success. So, find ways to share a laugh with those you lead and watch the dynamics around you shift for the better.

THE TAKEAWAY- KEEP THE HEALTHY LAUGHS ROLLING!

Although humor has many benefits, bear in mind that this only applies to good humor. Used correctly, humor can push a team to great heights. Used incorrectly, humor can cause more issues than it resolves. Let's discuss a few areas to avoid when sharing the gift of laughter with those you lead.

Don't act mimic an introvert or a new employee.
You'll come off as a tyrant instead of welcoming. Humor is not hurting someone's feelings or making fun of them.

Don't spread lies for the sake of amusement.
This is yet another example of sardonic humor. You will be greeted with laughter or ridicule, but you will also lose respect and be branded as a villain.

Don't be a narcissist.
Many people make fun of others, never themselves, and as a result, develop a superiority complex. This is also incorrect. You can make fun of others' flaws in a friendly/playful way as long as you still laugh at your flaws.

Don't go overboard.
Be wise enough to recognize that there is a time and place for fun. If you mess around all the time, you will come off as a clumsy idiot rather than a confident leader. It is not appropriate to spend all of one's time playing rather than working.

Laughter is the best medicine, as the saying goes. As a leader, find a way to leverage humor in your organization and work environment. Are you struggling to persuade someone to see your perspective? Try a little humor. It will take their attention away from being right, and they will become open to hearing your point of view. Are you smack dab in the middle of a heated argument with no hope of resolution? Try adding a touch of humor or a punch of a one-liner and see what happens. It will brighten the mood and encourage people to agree. Do you have a team member who is always forgetting an important step of a process? Instead of being harsh, try humor. They will remember the joke the next time they are in the middle of the process and remember the steps they should take. Are you feeling a little overwhelmed and stressed out? Are you having a hard time thinking through a challenging dilemma? Take a step back and find something to laugh about.

The benefits of humor are ENDLESS. Pinpoint healthy ways to incorporate humor into your personal and work life. And, if you are one of those people who laugh with their entire bodies, be careful as you laugh your way to the top of your success ladder!

Six

JUMP!

Everyone experiences fear. It is an emotion that sneaks into the heart of every leader, regardless of how successful they may be. Fear is most apparent when we think we're in the presence of or doing something that might cause us pain or injury -- physically, financially, etc. The presence of fear protects and prevents us from doing dangerous things. However, fear sometimes stops us from doing great things. Fear is why many people never embrace the leader within them. Leading in any capacity can be a rollercoaster ride of extreme emotions, and managing those emotions is just as important as creating the perfect product, making wise decisions for the expansion of an organization, or developing a solid business model. From my experience and from talking to other leaders on this journey, two key feelings that show up on a regular basis are fear and anxiety. In this chapter, we will deal with the components of fear that restrain leaders. My hope is that once you have completed this chapter, you will no longer allow fear to keep you from being the leader you know you can be. For leaders, there are many sources of fear, depending on the area in which they lead.

Entrepreneurs may wonder,
Can I make enough money to do this full-time?
Is my idea any good? Or, am I about to waste time and resources?

Organization leaders may wonder,
Will I create the impact I want?
Am I able to follow through?
What do I need to sacrifice?
What if I fail?

Corporate leaders may worry,
Will I have the support of my peers and superiors?
Will I change this company for the best?
What will people say about me once my time in this role is done?

Regardless of where we may lead, fear undermines our ability to move forward and make decisions. It narrows our perspective and makes us overthink our next step until we're overwhelmed with analysis paralysis. We tell ourselves that by reading more blogs and watching more inspirational TED talks, we will discover the perfect way forward. Instead, this remorseless over-analysis and blatant procrastination just overloads our senses and turns our brains to mush.

As leaders, we regularly deal with uncertainty and ambiguity. When you're doing something for the first time, you are never sure that you are doing the right thing. There are always unknown unknowns, which means you rarely have all the information you want. However, at some point, we must act, or else nothing will happen.

My daddy always said that his youngest son and his youngest daughter are willing to do anything and everything and ain't scared of crap! That would be Anthony and me. My brother Anthony was in the military, and he was part of the Airborne unit. He was accustomed to taking plunges, and you have to be fearless to do that. He would push every boundary he could without tipping over the edge or getting into too much trouble. Even to this day, he still rides his motorcycle, drives his corvette, embraces his inner daredevil!

The Anthony's in the world live by a different code. Rather than fear the outcome of what could happen if they "do," they fear the regret that could happen if they "don't." As a leader, know that the feelings of fear aren't abnormal. As I shared before, we all experience fear. What makes the difference is how we choose to respond to it.

You may not be as much of a daredevil as my brother, Anthony, but I believe that you have what it takes to fearlessly plunge into your lane, make daring decisions for your organization that will position you for success, and take leaps that others in your field have been afraid to take.

The Opportunity: Don't Wait Until It's Perfect. Just Do It!

Perfectionism fuels fear. Our desire to get things perfect before we jump supports the hold fear places on our decision-making skills. The bottom line is, if you want something out of life, you have to be fearless. Don't overanalyze the situation, as Nike says, *"Just Do It!"*

Perfectionism is described as the refusal to accept any quality less than perfection. It is an unquenchable desire to live up to your own or others' expectations of you. Desiring things to be perfect before you leap leaves you on the edge of the cliff, watching others jump and realize they could fly all along.

You don't have to get things right the first time, and it is okay to screw up. The most important thing is to move forward and learn from any mistakes or missteps along the way. If you have an idea for a new business, an innovative product, or a strategy for the company/organization, don't agonize over creating the perfect plan. Your instinct should be to share this imperfect idea with as many people as possible. Detach your self-worth from your ideas in order to be able to share them freely with others and those you lead without fear of being judged. Listen to their feedback, integrate what you hear, and improve your idea.

Too much of something, like too much of any natural force of nature (e.g., wind, fire, or water), can lead to chaos. Consider how the rain revives and gives fresh life to all it encounters as it rains on the earth. Excessive rain, on the other hand, can cause flooding and leave a path of destruction in its wake. For perfectionism, the same concept applies. The advantages of being meticulous, detail-oriented, careful, and competitive are well-known. The problem arises when achieving these goals does not result in a sense of happiness and fulfillment. Continuously trying to do it right and be the best will come at a high price and have negative consequences for your personal relationships, health, and well-being. I've worked with many successful leaders who readily admit to being perfectionists, aiming for the perfect life, perfect relationship, perfect body, perfect email, perfect picture, or to be the perfect student, perfect wife, perfect employee...*you catch my drift.* They are gifted individuals whose unwavering determination has enabled them to accomplish many great feats. Although others may be impressed by their accomplishments, they admit to being stressed and anything but flawless.

Aiming for perfection is doomed to bring pain, fatigue, and a sense of disappointment because it's impossible to achieve. There's no checkbox, no finish line, and no wrap party. (Even if perfection were possible, and there was a celebration, would there be anyone left for you to share it with?)

When you become conscious of something in your life and accept it, it loses its control over you. You are able to get back in the driver's seat and make deliberate decisions to adjust. Let's discuss a few ways leaders can stop allowing perfectionism to ruin their lives and fuel their fears.

Express gratitude.

Be thankful for what has happened and what you have already accomplished. Taking the opportunity to be grateful for how far you have come will fuel your boldness. Sometimes, all we need is a reminder of previous success to push us toward the next success.

Recognize the root of your perfectionism.

Investigate what motivates you to be a perfectionist. There's a reason you are trying to achieve perfection. Many people aspire to be ideal in order to satisfy a desire for love or to boost their self-esteem. I discovered that much of my own perfectionism stemmed from my fear of being rejected, despite the fact that it was ironically triggering the rejection I was trying to escape. Understanding why you desire perfection – no matter how difficult or problematic it becomes – will help you get to the root and deal with it.

Determine the ramifications.

Perfectionism can lead to low productivity, strained relationships, a loss of trust, anxiety, depression, and suicidal ideas. This self-discipline you take pride in will come at a price. When you recognize and consider the repercussions of your perfectionism, it motivates your mind to take action.

Perfectionism, if not understood and controlled, can limit you and those you lead. Be honest with yourself. What impact does perfectionism have on your health and well-being? Have you passed up chances to try something different because you were afraid you wouldn't be able to do it perfectly? Is your search for excellence causing conflict with your partner, children, or friends? How does this personality trait impact your coworkers?

Recognize that you are sufficient.

Many leaders criticize themselves for not being "enough"

of anything, such as attractive, fit, wealthy, efficient, at home, and so on. This is the voice of the inner critic. That little voice in your head that tells you that you are not good enough is incorrect! You are sufficient. You are more than sufficient. You were and will always be enough because you were born with it. Regardless of what you do or how perfect you are, you are worthy of love, success, happiness, and prosperity. Even if you don't believe it right now, a part of you knows it's real.

I understand how difficult it is. As a perfectionist, you see what's wrong before you see what's right. Instead of concentrating on what went wrong, why don't you remember what you are doing right? At the very least, do so before you try to work out how to change things in the future!

Always give it your everything.

My sister gave me several pieces of advice over the years. The piece of advice I depend on the most is, *"Do your best every day."* Isn't it simple? But, if you think about that, it's a very effective way to avoid being a perfectionist.

When you do your best, you will relax knowing that you have given it your all. You can live a life free of remorse. Sure, you'd like to do it differently next time, and there are probably some places where you can change, but that's just that — next time. Since you can't undo what's already happened, wasting resources on beating yourself up about it accomplishes little.

Allow yourself to let go, move on, and use your time and energy to make things better next time.

Accept failure.

I know you have heard numerous stories of successful people who used their mistakes to propel them forward. Walt Disney's editor said he "lacked creativity and had no interesting ideas," so he was fired from the Kansas City Star. Oprah Winfrey was told that she was "unfit for television." Michael Jordan once said, "In my career, I've missed over 9,000 shots. I've dropped nearly 300 games. I've been trusted to take the game-winning shot twenty-six times and failed. I've struggled many times in my life. That is why I am successful."

Most influential business leaders, founders, and athletes will tell you that failure has helped them succeed. Of course, accepting defeat is easier said than done. If you are growing and striving, you will struggle a lot in your life. You will make errors, screw up, and disappoint others. When this happens, accept that you made a mistake, but don't let the mistake become a part of your identity.

Appreciate your flaws.

What if your biggest flaw turned out to be your greatest asset? What if your adversity is really a source of strength? Consider all the great leaders you know who have triumphed over their flaws. Consider others who have influenced you in the past. Our shortcomings, as well as our ability to resolve challenges and fears, can also provide not only motivation and optimism but also a sense of community.

Take a step back.

It's likely that your perfectionism gets the best of you at times. You don't even know you're wasting time, money, or energy on something that doesn't have to be great, like a runaway train. Taking a step back allows you to breathe, reassess, and see your goals from a different angle.

Get to work and take action!

Waiting until you are positive things are perfect, and you are ready is a slippery slope to failure. To be honest, it's a kind of self-sabotage. We have a long way to go until we're ready and things are perfect. Yes, we should be prepared (don't just jump into the deep end of the pool if you haven't learned to swim yet). However, most of the scary opportunities leaders are presented aren't life or death. So, don't wait for trust to appear. Going for it is sometimes the best way to gain trust.

Desiring perfection works with fear to paralyze us. It causes us to drag our feet and put goals off for another day. We become prone to procrastination and fail to meet deadlines. Taking action is the single most important thing you can do to move past perfectionism.

THE TAKEAWAY: DON'T LET FEAR OF GETTING IT WRONG STOP YOU FROM TRYING TO GET IT RIGHT!

Fear of failure is a major obstacle for leaders. Though failure in leadership is undoubtedly avoidable, you will still have bumps in the road that may feel like failure. Goal setting and goal achieving go hand in hand, and they protect us from failure. We cannot allow fear should to put a stop to this. You simply need to know when to understand certain situations as failures or tests. Fear is simply a part of the natural human response to situations that are out of our control. That is not to say we should ever be afraid, but the sooner we realize that fear is only a response to the events that are outside of our control, the better off we will be. We can learn to let go of the fear quickly and to focus on the options at hand instead.

Fear isn't something you can control. It's something that you can learn to cope with and rationalize. When you are having irrational emotional reactions, use rational thoughts and focus on the things you can do to make things better.

Despite your fears, keep moving forward. Great leaders have fears; they just choose to press through them. Recognize that you are free to continue. Even when you're afraid, keep moving forward. Don't let it hold you down. Mark Twain once said, "Courage is resistance to terror, mastery of fear— not the absence of fear." Despite our worries, we must keep going forward. That is where we display our true bravery.

Aside from rock climbing, skydiving, and bungee jumping, the worst-case scenario is rarely as bad as it sounds in other cases. Recognizing the WORST case scenario will also help us understand that it's a lot less frightening and nebulous than we thought. So, what could possibly go wrong? It is possible that you would fail. You might lose your balance. It is possible that you will be injured. But, guess what? You get back on your feet. You can still bounce back, and the more you bounce back, the stronger you'll become.

Seven

PASS THE TISSUE!

My sister Twanda is the most emotional of all my siblings. We always tell her that she has leaky eye syndrome. I know there isn't such a thing, but she would definitely have it if there were! If she hears a story that has even the smallest amount of sadness, she cries. But once she gets herself together, she will be on a crusade to fix the problem.

I love that about Twanda because this is just an indication that she cares...deeply. Now, as a leader, I am grateful that I had this influence in my life. Tawanda is proof that you can be both productive and in tune with your emotions. In a time where so many believe you must be heartless to achieve success, emotional intelligence is a valuable skill to possess.

The Opportunity: Allow your emotions to work for you, not against you.

It's no secret that our emotions affect our decisions. Scientists have found that without emotions, we become completely ineffective at making decisions. Emotions also impact teamwork. That's a big reason why recent research shows emotional intelligence is one of the strongest predictors of success at work. The biggest problems arise when team decision-making and emotions collide.

When it comes to decision-making, a little emotion is good, even if the emotions seem inherently unpleasant or unproductive. Feeling a little fear, sadness, or irritation can help to spark motivation or broaden the search for alternatives.

On the flip side, a little too much emotion is generally bad, even if the emotions seem pleasant and productive. For example, when an entire team of people is feeling curious, excited, or confident, they are more likely to spend too much time admiring the view in their matching rose-colored glasses or happily making decisions that will drive the organization right off a cliff.

As we discussed in Chapter Two, having emotional intelligence helps us in decision-making. It allows us to be aware of how our emotions may impact our success and the success of those around us. Thus, developing a strong emotional intelligence will allow us to leverage emotions that drive us to solutions and reorient emotions that may cause us to act irrationally. As leaders, we must refrain from methods that encourage us to be emotionally intolerant and instead become more emotionally intelligent. This will allow us to lead better and be more effective and efficient at maximizing outcomes and desired results. Here are five methods you can use to become a more emotionally intelligent leader.

Care about people.

Caring is a simple thing to do, but it's not always expressed or genuine in its delivery or tone. Leaders need to balance the head and the heart. This means that leaders can't always be so intense about what is required from their teams.

Show that you care.

This method focuses on the actions you take because you care. There are many ways to show that you care. Take the time to mentor and/or sponsor people who have earned the opportunity. Ask about your employees' or team members' children or family. Follow up on difficulties they may be facing or things that may be impacting their lives. These simple gestures are more powerful than you might think in enabling you to achieve your leadership goals and objectives.

Intensity requires proper timing and focus to build and keep momentum.

As leaders, we need to show maturity along with our passion and be more compassionate to balance what the job requires with the human spirit.

Be Mindful of the Needs of Others.

If employees or team members are not working at or close to their capacity, you are not doing your job as a leader. Your sensitivity radar must always be on. This means that you are equally mindful of those you lead reaching their full potential as you are about yourself. Everyone has the ability to improve and increase their performance and productivity.

Help your team improve by providing continuous feedback, recommendations, affirmation, and suggestions.

Be a better leader and get the most production from your employees by giving them the feedback they need to succeed. If a team member needs to work on an area, let them know and give them tools to improve. If someone is doing a great job, highlight them, whether they are paid or volunteer staff. This is one of the greatest ways leaders can show that they are aware of the emotional needs of those they lead.

THE TAKEAWAY: EMOTIONALLY INTELLIGENT LEADERS ARE ALWAYS MORE SUCCESSFUL!

These days, employees and volunteers are much more conscious of whether or not they are a good match in an organization's culture. They desire leaders who are more aware of their needs. Team players are fed up with playing games and want to coexist in atmospheres that encourage them to be themselves. As a result, employees, in particular, manage their careers and seek advancement by looking for jobs that genuinely fuel their passion, satisfy their dreams, and ignite their true talent. The current economic climate has made career management even more difficult for most people. People also want their managers and representatives to be in tune with who they are as people (rather than only as coworkers) to ensure that their career path is in proper harmony with and respects their personal and professional interests. Regardless of where you lead, you must adjust to this if you desire to build strong teams.

Many leaders are so dependent on staying influential for their benefit that they have lost sight of how to better represent their workers (the people who help give them relevancy). Understand that as a leader, you become more valuable when you can demonstrate that you can maximize efficiency, employee/team engagement, and outcomes by fostering a collaborative atmosphere that encourages everyone to perform at their best.

Caring is a simple act, but it is not always articulated or sincere in its tone or delivery. Leaders must strike a balance between their heads and their hearts. As a result, leaders cannot always be as strict on what is expected of their workers. To create and maintain momentum, intensity necessitates proper timing and concentration. To reconcile what the job demands with the human spirit, we need to display wisdom alongside our zeal and be more compassionate as leaders. Those you lead don't want to be treated like cattle but rather as individuals valued for their hard work and effort. For the most part, people don't need their leaders to hold their hands; they just need to be aware of their responsibilities. People will perform if this is done with tact and good intentions.

Instead of transforming your teams to be more like you, focus on empowering employees and volunteers by showing them how their work will help their lives, not just the bottom line. Allow them to see and feel the human side of success to their families and lives outside of work. People nowadays want to feel as though they are making an impact to leave a mark on the world. Lead your team in ways that enable them to be both competitive and important at work.

The force that shifts people's lives and views on what matters most is significant. Make an extra effort to say thank you, and do so regularly. Take the time to mentor and/or support workers who have worked hard for their roles. Demonstrate that you care for others. Becoming more emotionally intelligent and acting on it will help you accomplish your leadership goals and objectives more effectively than you would expect.

Eight
YEP, I SAID IT!

We all need honesty, right? We need people to tell us the truth about everything, whether it is how we look in an outfit, if the meal we made tastes good, or if they think our partners are unfaithful. And, who do we turn to for honesty? Often, it's our friends and loved ones, though some are better at being honest than others. Some may tell us what they think we want to hear, while others may be blunt to the point of being hurtful.

Have you ever experienced anyone who doesn't have a filter and will say whatever? Well, that's my sister, Sylvia! Sometimes we are baffled at what comes out of her mouth at any given time, and she will defend herself by saying, "Well, they needed to hear it!"

Sylvia is extremely blunt and direct. I will stop short of saying she lacks emotion, but you will be hard-pressed to find any. She is the direct opposite of my sister, Twanda, – and they are right next to each other from an age perspective.

The good thing to know is that she is in no way trying to intentionally hurt you. She believes that being honest and blunt with people helps them a lot faster than lying to them.

People like my sister, Sylvia, just have a way of not sugar-coating something, and even if they never intend to be malicious, their words can still be hurtful. It may be challenging to find care and concern in the words of a blunt person. It's easy to feel judged but carefully consider their words. As a leader, you need people like this in your corner. Rather than feeling insulted, take some time to assess their words. Do they bring up a good point? Are they addressing something significant that you're avoiding? Is it possible that what they're saying hurts because there's some truth to it?

In addition to needing direct people in your circle, you will find that many of those you lead desire you to be direct. To many, having someone be direct with them is refreshing. Too often, we are tricked into believing a person feels one way about a situation when they really don't. A certain level of transparency and directness is necessary, so we don't go through life wearing rose-colored glasses. However, because we are emotionally intelligent leaders, we understand that there is a way to be direct without being rude. Mastering this ability will help us develop those around us. As those around us get better, we also become more successful.

THE OPPORTUNITY: BE DIRECT, NOT BLUNT.

Messages are communicated in a variety of ways by various people. Some are similar, whereas others are diametrically opposed. Being blunt works for my sister, Sylvia. However, as a leader, it might not work as well for you. As discussed in Chapter Seven, career and volunteer culture have shifted tremendously; people aren't tolerating rudeness from their superiors. Being blunt and rude may cause you to look around and realize you are working alone. As a leader, you must understand the subtle difference between being blunt and being direct. Being blunt is being honest, but often in a rude manner. Being direct is being honest and genuine while remaining diplomatic and respectful. They are both forms of honesty, but the difference is all in the tone and feel.

So, what are the most critical steps to take to be direct rather than blunt? How do we go about being extremely honest but not hurtful in our feedback?

Pay attention.

It's easy to come across as someone who has boarded a nonstop train and will continue to express their views regardless. If you're a frequently truthful and straightforward leader, keep in mind your true motivation: to express your thoughts and opinions directly without wasting time on pleasantries, vanity, or false praise.

It's important to remember to listen, observe, and truly understand the stance of others, especially before giving direct and constructive criticism. That way, when you give direct feedback, it will be helpful and contribute to both the organization's success and the employee/volunteer. If you don't consider this and other people's viewpoints simply to express your own, you'll be viewed as a jerk. Of course, this does not imply that you should remain silent; rather, you should listen & observe before speaking.

Try to be optimistic.

My mother always told me that it was okay not to like anything when I was a child. Yet, I felt compelled to explain why I didn't like it. Otherwise, it just seemed like I was moaning about something without suggesting a solution.

Being frank but not blunt can also be achieved by being positive. This demonstrates that you've considered a potential solution to whatever the issue is. If you're working on a project with a group of people, saying something like, "This concept is in utter shambles and makes no sense at all," can come across as harsh or offensive. However, if you claim, "This style is incomprehensible. To make this piece more cohesive, I believe we should add a third color," you would have expressed your opinion and suggested a solution to the problem you've identified. You're not only criticizing; you're still adding.

Concentrate on the task at hand rather than the person.

You've dealt with people who aren't used to a blunt tone and prefer a gentler touch and suggestions laced with compliments. As a result, they are unlikely to react positively or even understand how to respond to your directness. Focusing on the job or the issue at hand rather than the individual will go down easier in this case. You should base your comments on specifics, even if you don't wrap them in bubble wrap before expressing yourself. You'll appear less offensive as a result.

Instead of saying, "Your concept is completely nuts! That will never succeed," say, "That strategy isn't the best solution for achieving our target because...," or something similar. The argument is still being made, but no one's intellect is being insulted.

Watch your body language and tone.

You may have learned that words only make up a small part of a conversation and that tone and body language are more important. But, where did this come from? Professor Albert Mehrabian of the University of California, Los Angeles (UCLA), published Silent Messages in 1971. In Silent Messages, Mehrabian discusses his communication studies and the importance of tone and body language when talking to others. He says that the actual words we say only account for only 7% of what we communicate. Our voice (tone, intonation, and volume) accounts for 38 percent of communication, and our body language accounts for up to 55 percent. Mehrabian's model (7 - 38 - 55) is still widely used today.

Even though this study has been discussed and misinterpreted in the years after it was published, its core remains valid. When being straightforward, you must be aware of the tone you use and the body language you exhibit. For example, saying "No, that won't work" in a snappy tone while crossing your arms is not the same as saying the same thing in a neutral or thinking tone while keeping your arms uncrossed. Although the words themselves are the same (7%), the tone (38%) and body language (55%) are entirely different. The latter demonstrates that you gave the idea some thought (be it true or not).

THE TAKEAWAY: SUCCESSFUL LEADERS UNDERSTAND THE IMPORTANCE OF BEING DIRECT.

It is very unlikely to find "perfect" employees and volunteers who just know what to do at every juncture. Even individuals who are high-performers and self-motivated will need redirection now and then. How you handle these moments can make or break the momentum of your organization or business.

Being direct shows others their areas for improvement and helps them separate their self-value from what they need to improve to aid in the organization's success. It makes things objective. When not taken personally, direct construction criticism will help employees and volunteers distinguish exactly what needs to change. On the other hand, when suggestions are given and come off as angry, it could result in employees or volunteers feeling like they are the problem, rather than their actions or habits.

Remember to keep the spotlight of the statements on the actions you have observed, rather than labeling the person's character. For example, saying, "You are lazy," attaches a label. On the other hand, saying, "Your progress is slow," focuses on the visible behavior and does not make it a personal description.

When providing direct feedback, keep in mind to state what you have noticed. This leaves room for discussion, making your direct constructive criticism easier to accept. Instead of saying, "Your reports are late," approach it by saying, "I noticed that your reports are late." This gets the point across and paves the way for a healthy conversation.

If you are a more sensitive leader and are very careful not to hurt people's feelings, being direct can be nerve-wracking and understandably so. People come from different walks of life and have had different experiences, so knowing how to approach them can be difficult. On the other hand, you may be a very blunt leader and have realized that you need to create a healthier environment for your company's success. Whatever your leadership style, commit to mastering the ability to give necessary criticism in a direct and helpful way. The organization you lead depends on it.

Nine
A FRIEND IN NEED IS A FRIEND, INDEED!

Songs like "You've Got a Friend" by Carol King, "People Who Need People" by Barbra Streisand, and Joe Cocker's "With A Little Help From My Friends" express the critical role good friendships play in our lives.

Friendships are beneficial to one's welfare. Friends will help you celebrate happy occasions and offer comfort during difficult times. Friendships prevent isolation and allow you to have much-needed companionship. Having good friends boost your self-esteem, sense of purpose, and belonging. Friends help you navigate traumatic life events such as divorce, serious illness, work loss, or a loved one's death. The accountability found in solid friendships can improve your quality of life because good friends will encourage you to stop risky lifestyle patterns. Quality friendships also contribute to your physical health. Studies show that adults with a good social support network have a lower risk of depression, high blood pressure, and an unhealthy body mass index (BMI).

My life is proof of the many benefits of good friendships. Stacy is my ride-or-die sister and friend. After our older siblings moved out, Stacy and I were the last two in the house together. Naturally, we depended heavily on each other from a young age. We endured many difficult moments with our mom, so we always stuck together, and we are very close. It is said that the relationship siblings share is one of the most intense relationships that exist, with the most ups and downs. However, it's almost a law that a sense of unconditional love will prevail, one that forges a lasting bond and allows us to go through life's journeys together. My friendship with my sister, Stacy, taught me the value of having good friends and how to maintain those meaningful relationships.

THE OPPORTUNITY: MAKE AND MAINTAIN HEALTHY FRIENDSHIPS

Though friendships can significantly affect one's wellbeing, they are not always easy to form or sustain. Many leaders find it difficult to form new friendships or maintain established ones because other interests, such as employment or caring for children or elderly parents, may take precedence over friendships. Sometimes, changes in our lives or desires, relocating, getting a new job, or even a new love interest cause friends to drift apart. Once the dust settles, some people have become so accustomed to living without friends that they don't put forth the effort to rebuild or create new friendships. Without question, it takes effort to form and maintain healthy friendships, but the joy and comfort you receive from these friendships make the investment worth it.

In this section, we will discuss how to build new friendships and maintain current ones.

FRIENDSHIP MAINTENANCE

Giving and taking is an essential part of developing and sustaining healthy friendships. You may be the one providing assistance at times, and you may be the one seeking assistance at other times. Friendships remain strong when everyone feels cared for and valued despite who is on the receiving end in a particular season. Friendships stay healthy when both friends understand that it is just as important to be a good friend as it is to have a good friend. Here are a few ways to maintain your friendships.

Kindness is essential.

This fundamental behavior, which was stressed in childhood, is still at the heart of effective adult relationships. Consider friendship to be an emotional savings account. This account is credited for every act of kindness and expression of appreciation, although criticism and negativity deplete the account.

Pay attention.

Inquire into the lives of your friends. When you are on the phone or enjoying time with friends, give them your undivided attention. Eye contact, body language, and occasional quick statements like, "That sounds fun," let your friend know you are paying attention. Be sympathetic when friends share specifics of tough times or encounters, but don't offer advice unless your friend specifically requests it.

Be vulnerable.

True bonding comes from letting your guard down and allowing your true self to shine through. This can be a difficult task for many people. Being genuine necessitates a degree of vulnerability. It entails exposing our true selves, putting ourselves out there to be harmed, rejected, or judged. When you push past the desire to appear perfect, strong, and always together, you allow yourself to take advantage of the benefits authentic friendships offer. Sharing details about yourself builds intimacy with your friends. Allowing personal experiences and concerns to be shared demonstrates that your friend holds a special place in your life and strengthens your bond.

Demonstrate your ability to be trusted.

Trust is the foundation of all meaningful relationships. Breaching commitments is one of the surest ways to destroy confidence. If you consistently break promises, your credibility – and your relationships – will suffer. Forming good friendships requires being responsible and dependable. Keep your commitments and show up on time. Follow through on promises you've made to your pals. Keep personal information secret when you and your friends share it.

Spend intentional time with your friends.

It takes time — together — to develop a close friendship. Make an effort to see friends consistently and to keep in touch with them between get-togethers.

Making New Friends

Take a deep breath in. Now breathe out. Are you feeling better? As an adult, making new friends can be overwhelming. Depending on your age, most people have their BFFs for life and aren't interested in developing new friends. As a leader, you may struggle with feeling as if new opportunities at friendships aren't genuine. Your list of concerns about making new friendships is probably filled with fear of being rejected, embarrassed, or not knowing where to start. First, understand that no matter how many friends you currently have, your age, or your success, you should always be open to new friendships. Life is a journey, and along the way, we learn different things about ourselves. Meeting new friends on our path makes life a more fulfilling experience.

When it comes to friendships, quality is more important than quantity. Although having a diverse network of friends and acquaintances is beneficial for leaders, the goal should be to develop a few genuinely close friends who will be there for you in good times and bad. If you lack in the friendship department, know that there are many ways to develop new friendships. You've likely missed out on new mates already in your social circle. Consider people you've met — even if only briefly — who have left a good impression on you. You could make potential friends among:

- Former Co-workers or classmates.
- Former friends you haven't seen in a long time.
- Individuals you met at social events that you've enjoyed talking with

- Relatives

Reach out to someone who stands out in your mind as someone you'd like to learn more about. Request contact information from mutual friends or acquaintances, or — even better — reintroduce the two of you via text, email, or an in-person visit. Invite others to join you for coffee or lunch.

Visit places where others congregate to meet new people. Don't restrict yourself to a single approach to meeting new people. The greater your efforts, the more likely you are to succeed. Persistence is essential. Rather than waiting for invites to come your way, take the initiative and keep trying. Before you can say if your interest in a new friend is mutual, you may need to suggest plans a few times. Here are a few other suggestions for meeting new friends.

Participate in community activities.

Look for clubs or organizations that meet to discuss a common interest or hobby. These organizations are often advertised in newspapers and on neighborhood bulletin boards. There is also a slew of websites to help you meet new people in your neighborhood or area. Use words like [your city] + social network or [your neighborhood] + meet-ups in a Google search.

Become a volunteer.

Volunteer at a school, a place of worship, a museum, a community center, a charitable organization, or another organization. When you work with people who have common interests, you may form strong bonds.

Invite people and accept their invitations.

Invite a friend to coffee or lunch with you. Say 'yes' when you're invited to a social party. Then, return the favor by contacting someone who has recently invited you to an activity.

Take up a new hobby.

To meet people who share your values, enroll in a college or community education course. Participate in a wellness class at a nearby gym, senior center, or community center.

Join a faith-based organization.

New members can take advantage of special activities and get-to-know-you events.

Take a stroll.

Let your children or pet outside. Chat with other people who are out and about, or go to a famous park and start a conversation there.

Above all, keep a good attitude. Even if you don't make friends with everyone you meet, keeping a positive attitude and personality will help you strengthen your existing relationships and plant the seeds of friendship with new acquaintances. On your journey to improving your friendships, keep in mind that it's never too late to start making new friends or reconnect with old ones. Spending time making new friends and improving old ones will result in improved health and a more positive outlook.

THE TAKEAWAY: LEADERS NEED FRIENDS!

Hold on to true friends. They can be your most valuable asset as you move through various phases of your personal and professional life.

Knowing that you have a ride or die friend in your corner is sometimes all you need to get through this thing called life.

Every leader needs friends both in their industry and outside of it. With the right people around you, leading doesn't have to be as scary as some people make it out to be. Surround yourself with like-minded people who understand your emotional needs. Whether you want to make a global impact or just make a living, feeling connected to people who understand what you are going through makes uncertainty and ambiguity more bearable. Challenge yourself to be vulnerable and stop believing that you need to know it all and look like you're always in control. Leading in any capacity is challenging and can feel like we're constantly spinning plates, but there are many people out there feeling exactly the same!

When we authentically connect with others, we realize that the things we battle as leaders aren't abnormal. Suddenly the world feels less stressful because we know we're not alone.

If you know you have deficiencies in the friendship department, take charge to fix it. Yes, great friendships develop organically, but it still requires effort from both parties. Be the architect of your friendships rather than simply being a passenger. True friends anticipate spending time with you. If you haven't heard from them in a while, don't assume they're ignoring you; they're just as busy as you are. Don't be afraid of rejection, and don't take no for an insult. Simply schedule a meeting at a later time.

Our connected world allows us to make virtual friends worldwide, but real meaningful relationships go beyond likes and comments on social media. They necessitate thought and effort. Choose two or three close friends with whom to build authentic, meaningful relationships. Give your time and effort to them. It will greatly benefit your emotional, mental, and physical health.

Ten
BEAUTIFUL SURPRISES

When my husband Larry and I first started dating, I was a broken woman. I had been through a divorce, I was a single mom, and I was barely getting by trying to make a living. There were many things I wanted to do that I wouldn't have been able to do had he not been there to support and guide me through it all.

Larry helped me mend my heart and supported me as I became the strong woman I am today. We laugh about it now, but before we started dating, Larry had a checklist of things he wanted in a woman, and I didn't meet his criteria! But, we both learned that when you truly love someone, those things don't matter. You love them regardless, build each other up, and grow together. Larry and I have certainly grown and built a beautiful life together.

We are great business partners because we are totally opposite on some things, which always gives a different perspective when we are working through issues. Had we both adhered to the proverbial "checklist," we may not have ever found each other and embarked on this personal and professional journey together. If I had waited until I was perfect before I accepted his pursuit, I might have missed the opportunity to experience the healing of his love and support.

I didn't become the woman I am today with a beautiful marriage, amazing children, and a prosperous business because I could predict what would happen next in my life. Neither did it happen because I made all the perfect decisions or choices. I always knew what I wanted in life, but I had no idea it would come after a failed marriage, walking away from a great 9-5, and launching into uncharted territories as a business owner. What I endured to become who I am today was difficult and took a lot of effort to maneuver through. However, I'm a better woman because of it. More than anything, I am proud of myself for dreaming big and not allowing the difficulties to make me lose sight of my big dreams.

My marriage keeps me optimistic about the many beautiful surprises that may occur in life. Life is erratically unpredictable. I've learned that you can fly through life if you can adapt to the unpredictability of life. However, this is very difficult for many leaders because the mind can't help wondering what will happen in the future. Strong leaders know to prepare for the future they desire, but they remain ready to embrace the many unexpected twists, turns, and risks that life may present. Leaders who can embrace the unexpected aren't afraid of dreaming big. They know that unplanned events aren't detrimental to their big dreams. They are only obstacles that, with the right perspective, can present new opportunities for even greater success.

THE OPPORTUNITY: HONOR YOUR DREAMS

We are living in inspired times. While the job market and economy are always changing, there is still a path of deep security. It's your calling. You were born to excel in the work you love. It doesn't matter if you don't know how to find your calling or live it. Your brain might never know. But your instincts know nothing else. Your joy is your crystal-clear direction, not your detour.

Ditch the imprisoning mentality that your work must be validated or franchised or net a certain amount of money to be worth it. Truly, you can't even imagine the opportunities and the serotonin boosts of clarity that will come with pursuing what you love. So often, our joy takes us by surprise and expands our definition of who we think we are and what we think is possible.

Dreaming big dreams is the first step toward any type of success. Do you desire financial freedom? Dream big! See yourself receiving the letter that all your debt has been paid off. Do you desire to be an actor? Dream big! See yourself on billboards and posters. Do you desire to make an impact in politics? Dream big! See yourself sitting at the table with the movers and shakers of the world. Success begins with big dreams! Don't restrict yourself to what seems to be the most realistic or traditional. You have a lot of talent, and the possibilities are limitless for you. Dream big and think beyond the cage! It is up to you to shape your future.

Some people never succeed in anything for the simple reason that it never occurs to them that they can. As a result, they never attempt. They never get going. They continue to go in circles with their money, wasting everything they earn and a little more. However, when you start dreaming big dreams, you see yourself and your life in a different light. You gradually begin to do different things, and, bit by bit, your entire life path changes for the better.

You are a doer, an innovator, and a game-changer with distinct passions and lofty ambitions! When you dream big, the prospect of achieving your objectives becomes completely overwhelming. But don't worry, you've got this. Nothing is too large to achieve, no matter how overwhelming the goals seem to be.

So, where do you begin? Start small because—believe me—there are no small steps. Every step you take to honor your dreams is huge. Take 10 minutes to sing, write, meditate, or brainstorm about your vision. Start the inquiry this very second. Honor your gifts, and you will honor your lifetime!

Take a chance on yourself!

Millions of people have brilliant ideas, but only a small percentage of them have the desire and ambition to see them manifest. You must be willing to put everything on the line. Put your fears of failure to the side and take a chance. Rather than pondering the "what-ifs," just go for it and take the first steps toward realizing your vision. You don't need to have all of the nuances and decisions completely ironed out to get your project off the ground. Along the way, kinks can be worked out. Make the best decision you can based on the information you have. Rather than losing out on the chance to make something amazing, take a chance.

Get the right help.

Be intentional as you envision the team or support you need to get your dream off the ground. Don't confuse excellent people with people who are exceptional in what they do. Look for people who are well-rounded and share your interests. They will guide you in the right direction through good, poor, and ugly times. With anything new, every player involved may have to do more than what is stated in the job description, especially in a start-up business. The truth is, you don't really know what you need yet. Ensure that everyone involved is aware of this and willing to grow as what you are building grows. When recruiting a close friend, however, be cautious. I learned the hard way not to recruit a friend simply because I like them. Be frank with yourself about your friend's abilities and willingness to put in the effort.

Make difficult choices.

"Advice is something you ask for when you already know the answer but wish you didn't," Erica Jong once said. Only by taking chances and making tough decisions can you achieve success. There isn't an easy way out. Trust your instincts. Have faith in your ability to determine what is best for your dream. Be confident in your choices. There's no time for second-guessing yourself.

Appreciate the small wins.

All leaders strive for historic achievements, but they must remember to live in the moment. Recognize your small victories as you progress. Taking the time to focus on the little stuff would raise morale and contribute to developing a strong culture in what you are building.

Visualize your objectives.

It is important to have big dreams. However, if you don't have a good idea of what you want, turning those visions into reality would be far more difficult. Using a vision board to chart your goals gives your wild imagination a bit more structure. Vision boards will help you stay motivated and inspired to achieve your objectives. Though vision boards can serve as a roadmap for your future, the best thing about them is that they aren't set in stone; you can change them as much as you want without losing their effectiveness.

Take breaks when necessary.

Leaders are under a lot of pressure to not only make wise decisions but also work for that goal constantly. Give yourself a break if you're tired from your daily routine. Practicing a five-minute idle interval during times of high stress will help you recharge and refocus. Don't let yourself get burned out, and don't feel bad if you take a break.

Don't make comparisons to anyone.

It can be discouraging to see your peers achieve big milestones, particularly when your achievements seem to be slipping through your fingers. It's almost impossible to resist comparing yourself to others, but try not to let it bother you. Negative self-talk should be replaced with optimistic affirmations, and jealousy should be replaced with appreciation. Celebrating even the tiniest wins gives you the confidence boost you need to tackle the next challenge.

Don't get defeated by minor setbacks.

You can make the most comprehensive plan for your future, but you never know when life will throw you a curveball. Don't let a little disappointment throw you off track, whether it's a sluggish day at practice or a rejection from an opportunity you were hoping for. These setbacks may be discouraging in the short term, yet they also provide excellent opportunities to learn and develop. A move away from your ideal path can often turn out to be a step in the right direction.

Make use of your network.

Though your dreams are special to you, you are not alone in pursuing them. Always keep in mind that you have friends, family, coaches, instructors, and mentors to support you. Never be afraid to seek assistance or advice; your community cares for you and wants you to excel just as much as you do.

THE TAKEAWAY: YOU DESERVE TO BE HAPPY!

There is no greater feeling than defeating the odds, laying it all on the line, and going full-speed ahead after the dreams in your heart. As you chase the dreams that make your heart beat fast, keep in mind that your success is determined not just by tangible indicators (compensation, title, reputation) but also by the underlying enjoyment you derive from what you do.

Happiness is a subjective concept; one person's happiness can not make another feel the same way. However, even though our definitions of happiness are subjective, there are some simple necessities that we all need to live a happy life.

WELL-BEING

The most significant aspect of happiness is your well-being. Happiness necessitates not only physical but also mental and emotional well-being. Your chances of happiness dwindle if you don't have these three types of well-being. You're surviving rather than living. It is important to maintain your overall health. Make every effort to maintain your physical, mental, and emotional well-being. A person's well-being is a priceless asset.

MONEY

Money is undoubtedly one of the most divisive aspects of happiness. We've all heard the adage that money can't buy happiness over and over again. It's generally said by people who seem to have made a very happy life for themselves because they have a lot of money!

To be happy, you don't have to be a billionaire, but having a certain amount of money will help you have a more optimistic outlook on life in general. It provides you with a safety net. When a minor financial crisis strikes, you don't have to worry about not being able to make your mortgage payments, losing your house, not having enough money to fix your vehicle, or feeling desperate. Getting enough money to take care of yourself and those you care for is unquestionably reassuring. Money isn't bad in and of itself, and it's necessary. It can give you more time to fulfill your goals and dreams, and there's nothing wrong with living a lifestyle that makes you happier.

RELATIONSHIPS

As we discussed in Chapter Nine, you don't need 50 BFFs to be content, nor do you need to be a member of any online social network. People who care for you and vice versa are all you need in your life. People you can laugh with, weep with, embrace, touch, kiss, and share life with. Statistics have consistently shown the advantages of having stable relationships in life, whether with friends or in a romantic partnership. We should include our pets in this category because they are constant companions who love us unconditionally.

WORKPLACE CONTENTMENT

Keep in mind the word contentment. You don't have to love your job to be satisfied with it, but you should be able to enjoy it for the majority of the day. Will you be frustrated for days? Yes, absolutely! However, your work can be more than just a source of income for you.

Make strong plans to quit if you are in a position that you really despise (and we've all been there at one point or another). Continue looking for the work you want, be open to new opportunities, and maintain a positive attitude. Find a sliver of heaven in your hell, and remember that it's just for a while. Life does not remain static until you give up.

SELF-RESPECT & SELF-ACCEPTANCE

Self-love has a poor reputation because it is often confused with the term selfish. Between the two terms, there's a world of difference. True happiness necessitates love and acceptance of oneself. You're on your way to a happier life if you embrace yourself for who you are, flaws and all. This isn't to say that you won't continue to make changes in your life; rather, it means that you understand who you are, your strengths and limitations, and want to do what is best for you to live a good and happy life.

The right to happiness is a fundamental right. Simply because you are alive, you deserve to be happy. The definition of happiness, on the other hand, varies from person to person; we are, after all, individuals. The five essentials of health, wealth, relationships, work contentment, and self-acceptance, on the other hand, form the foundation for finding happiness for yourself. Put them to use and see what a difference they make in your life.

So, what are you waiting for? You won't bring much meaning to your life if you repeat the same life experiences repeatedly. If you don't explore life, it becomes dull and boring. Honor your dreams, set goals for the success you desire, and embrace life's unexpected twists and turns. I've got a good feeling that several beautiful surprises are awaiting your much-anticipated arrival!

FINAL WORD FROM THE AUTHOR

As I look back on everything that I gleaned from my siblings and husband, I realize that I am a sum of these parts. I am a chameleon, and I embrace that about myself. I am constantly changing and evolving as things change and evolve in my life. I tend to work on a problem until I solve it, and then once I solve it, I am on to the next thing. I don't like to remain stagnant in a situation; that is why I describe myself in this way.

In life, we have to be able to adapt to whatever situation we find ourselves in. That's not to say we have to change who we are at the core, but that is to say that we have to read and know those we lead and be able to stand and deliver what the situation calls for.

Often, we know what we want and deserve, but we constantly find ourselves in situations where we have to prove that we deserve it. As leaders, we have to always be mindful that there are certain things that we have to embrace to put ourselves on a path that leads to greatness. The ability to effectively understand and embrace the characteristics of friends and family and leverage them in our own lives is critical to business success.

I am powered by 10....*what's your source of power?*

ABOUT THE AUTHOR

Kim Caudle Lewis is the Chief Executive Officer of PROJECTXYZ, Inc., a business that provides services and products in the areas of engineering, logistics, technology, manufacturing, alternative energy, and international foreign military sales. She leads a workforce that supports federal and commercial customers across seven diverse subsidiaries and at locations across the United States and around the world. Lewis has a 25-year career spanning business operations and management, technology, and federal government contracting.

A life-long resident of North Alabama, Lewis would later become the first black female elected as Board Chair of the Huntsville/Madison Chamber of Commerce and most recently, the first black female owner of North Alabama's only locally owned broadcast television station, WTZT-TV.

Lewis' previous career roles and studies in healthcare and information technology set the foundation for starting

PROJECTXYZ and where she was previously involved in management of IT implementations and projects for large healthcare companies. She earned a degree in Computer Information Systems at John C. Calhoun State Community College.

HONORS, AWARDS, & RECOGNITION

- Russell Brown Executive Leadership Award Huntsville/ Madison Chamber of Commerce 2020
- Women of Impact for Alabama, Yellowhammer Media 2019
- Women of Distinction, Girl Scouts of North Central Alabama
- Women that Shape the State, Alabama Media Group
- Women's Economic Development Council Women Honoring Women Award 2017
- College of Business Fellow, University of Alabama, Huntsville 2020
- US Department of Defense Nunn-Perry Mentor Protégé Award
- US Chamber of Commerce Women-Owned Business Achievement Award
- US Chamber of Commerce Blue Ribbon award
- Huntsville/Madison Chamber Small Business of the Year
- Inc. 5000 Fastest Growing Companies − 2014; 2015; 2016; 2017; 2021

CURRENT BOARD APPOINTMENTS

- Tennessee Valley Authority Board of Directors- pending Senate Confirmation
- Huntsville Utilities
- Cummings Research Park Board, Huntsville, Alabama
- Crestwood Medical Center, Huntsville, Alabama
- The Shoals Chamber of Commerce
- Public Affairs Research Council of Alabama (PARCA)
- Women Economic Development Council Foundation
- University of Alabama Huntsville (UAH) Foundation
- John C. Calhoun State Community College Foundation
- Health Establishments at Local Schools (HEALS)

PREVIOUS APPOINTMENTS

- Huntsville/Madison Chamber, Board Chair
- National Children's Advocacy Council, Board Chair
- Unity Negro College Fund Committee (UNCF), Chair

PERSONAL

Lewis is married to Larry E. Lewis, Jr who joined PROJECTXYZ in 2007 as President. She has two daughters, Sandi and Lela and one grandson, Elijah.

CONNECT WITH THE AUTHOR

Thank you for reading, *Power of Ten: Opportunities Every Leader Should Leverage.* Kim can't wait to connect with you! Here are a few ways you can contact the author.

FACEBOOK   KIM CAUDLE LEWIS

INSTAGRAM   @KIMCAUDLELEWIS

WEBSITE   KIMCAUDLELEWIS.KIM

EMAIL   KIM@KIMCAUDLELEWIS.COM

Made in the USA
Columbia, SC
20 February 2022

56215126R00069